T0380967

LOST
ON
LIBERTY
ISLAND

JER
Illustrated by Ashlynn Simpson

Print information available on the last page

Rev. date: 01/15/2020

To order additional copies of this book, contact:
Xlibris
1-888-795-4274
www.Xlibris.com
Orders@Xlibris.com

"Good morning, wake up! Today will be a special day guess what we're going to see?" the father softly whispers.

"Come on everyone, so we can catch the train it leaves in 30 minutes." as he hurried everyone up and out the house.

"Mom, why do we have to get up so early where are we going" everyone asked.

"We're going to see the Statue of Liberty so, let's get a move on it."

"Can we go to the park?" Lexy asked as they walked passed.

"We will go to the park on another day as long as it's sunny out." the mother replied as she smiled.

"We are at our stop just in time to catch the second train and next will be the ferry" the Dad says.

"Come on, let's keep moving" Aunt Liz huddled the kids along.

"We can all grab something to eat at the next stop" mom softly replies.

"Look there is a circus in town, I want to go mom it will be fun!" Isaiah and Lexy excitedly exclaimed.

"Will the circus have lions and tigers?" Isaiah asked.

"Yes, and there should be clowns, music and rides too, we will save that for another day."

"Mom, we're hungry, how much longer before we can get something to eat?" the children asked.

"The next stop will come soon, what do you want to eat?" mom asked "There's Chinese, Mexican, McDonald's and Subway"

"Can we have some Chinese please?" and off went to eat their afternoon lunch.

"Don't take too long we still need to catch the ferry" mom said as everyone began to eat.

Sean saw that everyone had finished eating, so everyone walked towards the ferry.

"Dad are we getting on this boat it's big" the kids asked with excitement in their voice.

"Yes, it's time to catch the ferry to Liberty Island" dad replied.

"I can't wait to see the Statue of Liberty!"

As everyone walked onto the busy ferry the family headed upstairs to enjoy the view.

As Isaiah turned to his dad he said, "it's so nice up here you can see everything."

"Would you like to see the front of the boat?" father replied.

"Yes dad" as the two walked to the front of the boat the rest of the family was inside the ferry in the covered room.

"Mom where are dad and Isaiah going? I want to go with them too?" Lexi asked.

"Ok, let's go!" as they walked in the same direction as Sean and Isaiah.

"The wind is blowing out here mom and the waves are low" Lexi expressed.

"Can you swim in the water?" she asked her mom.

"No, this water is really cold and a lot of boats are out here" the mother replied.

"Look over here mom, what is that in the water" Lexi asked her mother.

"I can't see anything Lexi but look, we are near the Statue of Liberty" mom said.

"Sean, Isaiah we are close to the Island" the mom said.

"Let's stay together when were on the Island" father said.

"Isaiah did you see anything in the water?" mom asked.

"No, dad was showing me the boat engine and we saw other boats passing by" he replied.

"Were here now take your time getting off the ferry so you don't fall and I have Licia" mom said.

"Look Licia, the big statue can you see it" she shook her head yes as her eyes grew bigger with excitement.

"Mom, can I go with Auntie Liz" Lexi asked her mom.

"Ok, but make sure not to let go of your Aunt hand this is a big island" both parents replied.

"Aunt Liz do you mind Lexi being with you?" mom asked.

"Not at all, we will be over here at the shops" Aunt Liz replied.

Off the rest of the family went to explore the island.

"Look Isaiah and Licia how big the statue looks now that we are so close!" mom said.

As Isaiah looked up at the statue he said "I'm so little and the statue is very big mom and dad."

Sean replied, "Yes, and it took a lot of people a very long time to build it."

Walking around the Island and learning the history was fun family time.

As time passed by the family decided it was time to find Aunt Liz and Lexi.

"Aunt Liz, it's getting pretty late, we are ready to head back" J expressed.

"Where is Lexi Aunt Liz?" mom asked.

With a puzzled look on her face, she replied "she walked to you."

Just then, everyone was worried the Island is big and there were a lot of people visiting.

"I'm sure she will be ok" mom expressed "she knows to look for the police," dad replied.

A few minutes had passed and they could not find Lexi.

Mom walked back to the shop where the Aunt and daughter were.

Standing there with a policeman was Lexi, looking around the crowd.

"Officer, thank you for finding my daughter" a relieved look on her face, mom was happy.

"Everyone was so worried because the island is big and there were a lot of people" the mom said as she hugged Lexi.

"She was a brave kid Miss." the officer said "she was able to tell us her name."

"I knew you would find me" Lexi said in a soft tone.

As the two walked back to the rest of the family the mom held her hand tight.

"Daddy" Lexi yelled as she ran and jumped into his arms.

"Are you ok Lexi?" Isaiah asked his little sister.

Licia just looked as she was too young to know what was going on.

The family was back together again and walked towards the ferry to go home.

"Lexi, what happened that you lost your Auntie?" mom asked concerned.

"I was walking to you and then you were gone, then I walked back to Auntie and she was gone" Lexi replied.

"Mom, I saw the policeman and asked him for help" Lexi stated.

"I'm glad you had the officer there to help you" mom replied as she kept hugging Lexi.

"Mom, the officer asked me your name and I said Mom is that wrong" Lexi asked.

The mom smiled and replied "yes, I'm your mom and I do have a name."

"I'm just glad we are back together again" mom said smiling as she continued to hug Lexi.

As they walked towards the ferry Lexi says, "I will not forget this trip mom."

As the mom continued holding Lexi's hand then turns and smile as the sun begins to set she replies "neither will I my daughter."

And off in the distance the ferry boat driver says, "Next stop, Battle Park."

Match word with Picture

Ferry

Lady Liberty

New York

Park

Police

Tourist

Train

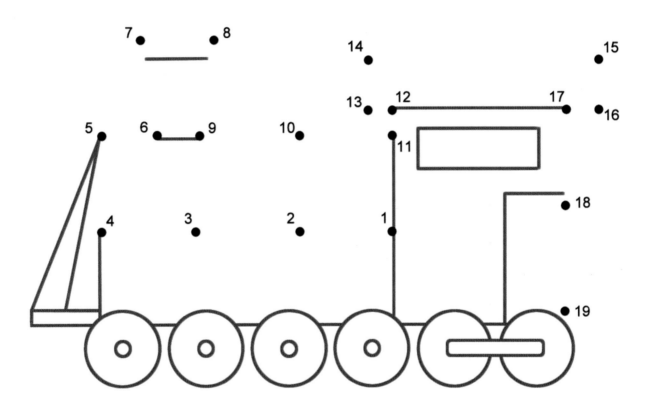

Unscramble Words

_____ fryer

_____ ayld teryibl

_____ wne roky

_____ kapr

_____ iploec

_____ utsirot

_____ narit

This book is dedicated to the Men & Women of Law Enforcement and my Military Security Forces Defenders. Thank you, New York Police Department, for helping my daughter feel safe and finding her parents when she was lost on Liberty Island. She was able to communicate without fear. Thank you to all of Security Forces Defenders for protecting us and showing us love and doing what you do best!

Gate 1 Bagram AB 2009 with 455 SFS & CMSAF Roy in the middle.

While attending nursing class as a Reserve SNCO, I stop to see off a Team of Defenders.

CSAF and CMSAF visit Eglin AFB

Alaska Air Force Base

CMSGT Visit Eglin AFB

Afghanistan 2011, First USAF Security
Forces Female Engagement Team.
Traveled to villages of Parwan
Province to encourage mothers
and children to be safe.

Security Forces Defender

Printed in the United States
By Bookmasters